Connor Court Quarterly
Volume 17

Saint Gregory of Nyssa
On the Soul and the Resurrection

Brian Ephrem Fitzgerald

Connor Court Publishing

Published by Connor Court Publishing Pty Ltd, 2024

Copyright © Brian Ephrem Fitzgerald

CONNOR COURT PUBLISHING PTY LTD
PO Box 7257
Redland Bay QLD 4165
sales@connorcourt.com
www.connorcourtpublishing.com.au

ISBN: 9781923224032

Cover design by Ian James
Printed in Australia

PREVIOUS ISSUES OF
THE CONNOR COURT QUARTERLY

Volume 16
Woke Capitalism and the Power of Ideas

Volume 15
The chattering classes, whispering classes, bully-victims and cancel-culture: life and education in the politically correct era

Volume 14
Intelligent Design: Interview with Bill Dembski

Volume 13
Covid19 - The Role of the State

Volume 12
Was Australia Discovered by De Quiros in the Year 1606

**Visit online to get your copy:
www.connorcourtpublishing.com.au**

Saint Gregory of Nyssa
On the Soul and the Resurrection

Brian Ephrem Fitzgerald

Saint Gregory of Nyssa: His Life

St. Gregory of Nyssa, the younger brother of St. Basil the Great (c. 330-379) was born around 330 and was educated chiefly by Basil. Like his older brother, he opted at first for a secular career in rhetoric. Unlike Basil, he even married. Under the influence of his friends, especially St. Gregory of Nazianzus (c. 329-389), he retired to the same monastery on the Iris which his brother, St. Basil, founded.

In 371, his ecclesiastical career advanced further, being elevated to the episcopal seat of Nyssa (in modern central Turkey), a small town in St. Basil's metropolitan district of Caesarea. Unlike St. Gregory of Nazianzus, St. Basil's brother actually went to his see and stayed there, although he was elevated against his will.[1] Not being the able administrator that St. Basil was, St. Gregory disappointed his brother, who frequently faulted the latter for his political ineptitude and his lack of firmness in dealing with people.

St. Gregory of Nyssa was no financial wizard either, and St. Basil criticized him for this. Even worse, his Arian opponents exploited Gregory's financial administrative slackness to manufacture charges of misappropriating Church funds. In 376, while St. Gregory was absent, a synod of Arian bishops and court prelates gathered in Nyssa and deposed him. In 378, after the death of the Arian emperor Valens, St. Gregory returned to his see in Nyssa.[2]

A year later, St. Gregory attended a Synod at Antioch

and was subsequently sent by the synod as a visitor to the diocese of Pontus. While there, he was elected archbishop of Sebaste (380) which he had to administer for a few months, although much against his will.

In 381, together with St. Gregory of Nazianzus, St. Gregory of Nyssa, took a prominent role at the Second Ecumenical Council in Constantinople wherein the trinitarian dogmas of Nicene Orthodoxy prevailed. He visited the capital frequently afterwards. In 385 he delivered a funeral oration for the princess Pulcheria and, not much later, that of her mother, the empress Flacilla, as well. The last time he appeared in Constantinople was in 394 for a synod called by the Patriarch Nectarios. Apparently he died soon afterward. The Orthodox celebrate his memory on 10 January.[3]

An administrator and politician he may not have been, but among the Cappadocian Fathers he was perhaps the deepest thinker and most versatile author. He was less restrained in his use of the literary motifs of his day and clearly displayed a more positive evaluation of contemporary philosophical thought. Atticisms abound in his works, but, as a Christian theologian, he is hardly shy in citing either the common Greek of the New Testament or the Greek of the Septuagint (henceforth LXX). Although he accepted the influence of contemporary Hellenistic rhetoric, he was never its master.[4]

His often less-than-charming literary style did not prevent

him from becoming perhaps the foremost thinker and theologian of the Cappadocian Fathers. Together with St. Gregory of Nazianzus, St. Gregory of Nyssa helped develop fully the trinitarian theology and terminology of his elder brother, St. Basil the Great. At the Second Ecumenical Council in Constantinople, together with St. Gregory of Nazianzus, he led in advocating the official adoption of Nicene trinitarian thought. His vision of Christian divinization is perhaps one of the most inspiring elaborations of this concept. His philosophical and intellectual broad-mindedness together with his very positive evaluation of Greek literature gave him perhaps a certain flexibility and originality not seen in the other Cappadocian Fathers.

About 'On the Soul and the Resurrection'

After St. Basil's death in early 379, St. Gregory of Nyssa visited his sister, St. Macrina, at the convent on the Iris where she was the abbess. Here he sought consolation concerning the recent loss of his brother, only to find that his sister too was soon to die. His deathbed discussions with her concerning the immortality of the soul and the Resurrection apparently raised his spirits greatly.[5] St. Macrina died the next day and St. Gregory probably composed *On the Soul and the Resurrection* shortly afterwards.[6]

Modeled upon the deathbed dialogue of Socrates in

Plato's, *Phaedo*, St. Gregory composes a deathbed dialogue between St. Macrina and himself wherein he plays the "devil's advocate" while St. Macrina presents the proper Christian understanding concerning the immortality of the soul and the hope of the Resurrection. The ideas attributed to St. Macrina, naturally, are those of the author himself. Holy Writ is utterly authoritative in Christian theology. But St. Gregory confesses that, since what Holy Writ posits is to be accepted as divine commands, the soul lacks a certain assurance which comes from reasoning out an issue thoroughly. Hence he finds his own faith standing, but without the level of assurance he would desire, leaving his soul distraught at the recent departure of St. Basil and at the immanent departure of St. Macrina.[7]

In this deathbed discussion, St. Macrina and St. Gregory reason out the philosophical underpinnings of the Christian's hope. Holy Writ is the authoritative source of Christian theology, but human reason enlightened by the Holy Spirit can supplement one's theological endeavors and thus bolster one's faith. Reason, therefore, serves as a handmaiden to theology which can buttress one's faith when it wavers as did St. Gregory's. This method reveals the work's primary audience, namely a Christian one.

As a result, this work displays quite well St. Gregory's philosophical and literary learning. It also serves as an example of the positive role secular learning can play in Christian life and thought. This work therefore displays much of the *flexibility* toward contemporary Greek though and literary style discussed above. Due to the nature of this work, theological anthrolopogy plays a key role, especially concerning the nature of the human soul in its relationship to the human body and to the divine nature. The theological anthropology which underlies this book will prove very influential in later Orthodox Christian ascetical and theological writings. This, however, will be discussed in greater depth later.

The Nature of the Soul

The cause of St. Gregory's anxiety, as presented in this work, are his doubts about the immortality of the soul. In this debate, he begins by raising two objections concerning this issue: a) assuming that the soul is complex and composed of the same elements as the body, it is dissolved in death together with the body, and b) if the soul is of a different nature than the body it cannot be in it and if it is not in the body it cannot exist at all since there is no other place where it could be. This assumes that for the soul to exist in the body it must have the same nature as the body. Here the soul would exist only until the dissolution of the body in death. But if the soul does not share the body's nature, it cannot exist at all since it cannot then be in the body and there is no other place for it in the universe.[8]

St. Macrina discredits these objections as being opinions

held by the Stoics and Epicureans.[9] The latter she accuses of understanding nature to be fortuitous, automatic, and without providential oversight. Appearance therefore defines nature and sensation is the means to knowing it. Such opinions, she believes, are the results of a spiritual blindness which comes from excluding the intellectual realities which are known only by the mind. For these "small-souled" people, perceptible things no longer point to deeper realities but become walls obscuring any vision of things intellectual. Hence they see only the elements of which the universe is made and are unable to infer from the skillful designs therein the existence of its invisible designer. After all, if one perceives a house, should not one's mind infer from it the carpenter who built it, or from a ship the shipwright, or from a garment the weaver?[10]

Such views assume that the soul is either made of physical elements, as is the body, with all the attributes of physical things, i.e., mass, dimension, complexity, and so forth. Two things cannot occupy the same space, so the soul must be of the same elements as the body or nowhere. St. Macrina disavows these notions. As far as she is concerned, let those who assume the soul to be nowhere since it differs in nature from the body also assume bodily life to be soulless.[11] On the other hand, let them not speak of the soul as being within the bodily elements giving them life if the soul does not continue to exist after death as do the elements. Given either argument, what would distinguish life from death? If they say that the soul dwells in the body but does not survive the body's death, let them say the same thing about the divine nature itself! But such a proposition would abolish the very divinity who is in the universe and maintains it and therefore divine providence.[12]

The skillful design and harmony of the visible universe proclaims its Maker.[13] If one transcends one's mere senses, he can perceive intellectually a skillful and wise divinity who created, maintains and permeates all things. St. Gregory accepts this idea, but questions how accepting the existence of God implies the existence of the soul since God and the soul are not the same. St. Macrina responds that man is a microcosm of the universe.[14] With the senses one perceives the sensible universe and thereby infers the reality and intelligence which surpasses the senses. If one examines the universe within oneself, he finds a good place to learn about the soul. Analysis of the visible infers the invisible. The Christian confirms thereby that the soul exists in itself, having a nature which differs from the body's solidity.[15]

What else does one learn from this examination? The soul is intellectual, immaterial, bodiless, invisible, living and vivifying. The soul works in accordance with its own nature and reveals its motions through bodily organs. The same arrangement of elements can be seen in living bodies and corpses, but with regard to corpses the soul remains immobile and inactivated. The soul is activated only when perception resides in the organs and intellect pervades perception, moving the organs of perception according to its own voluntary impulses. Human sensation therefore reveals the indwelling, effective, intellectual, and vivifying presence of the soul. Upon St. Gregory's request, St. Macrina defines the soul as follows:

> *The soul is an essence which has a beginning; it is a living and intellectual essence which by itself gives to the organic and sensory body the power of life and reception of sense impressions as long as the nature which can receive these maintains its existence.*[16]

The intellectual capacity to extrapolate realities invisible to the senses but inferred from what they perceive confirms the verity of this definition. How else would one know, for example, that the sun is much larger than it appears to the senses, even many times larger than the earth, unless the underlying intellect discerned this from observation and declared it so? How would one know that the moon revolves around the earth, receives its light from the sun, and so forth, except by reasoning it out from observing its waxing and waning? The intellect, which is a property of the soul, infers from what is seen that which is unseen. After all, invisible geometric principles are extrapolated from the observation of sensible figures.

But how would this be possible if no intellectual power was present in the sensory organs? In support of this notion, St. Macrina cites Epicharmus to the effect that it is the mind which both sees and hears.[17]

St. Gregory turns to the issue of human locomotion and points out that men have devised machines which, through the nature of their elements and artful arrangement, move, make noise, and so forth. Yet nobody would posit an intellectual power in them. Might this not also be true of human nature? Might it not be that a kinetic, and not an intellectual power, drives human nature? Yet in these contraptions, St. Macrina finds further evidence of the invisible and intellectual essence of the soul. Someone had to study these elements, reason out how to arrange them, and assemble them artfully to achieve the desired effect. This must prove that in man there is a mind which is beyond what is visible. By the intelligence of its own nature the mind devises such things by thought and manifests the concept within through the assistance of the materials used to construct it. If some invisible intelligence did not underlie such devices one would expect such things to arise spontaneously in nature. Since that never happens, one can extrapolate from them the existence of the invisible intellectual essence within the man who designed them.[18]

St. Gregory now objects that all this proves is what the soul *is not*, i.e., it is not visible, not dimensional, not material, and so forth. But the question is what the soul *is*. St. Macrina replies that much is learned from negative assertions, even the very being of the thing being pondered. Goodness is presented as *not evil*. The nature of cowardice is well revealed in the term *unmanliness*. One can understand the nature of better qualities through the denial of the worse, and vice versa, the nature of evil by the deprivation of good qualities. Since the soul can be inferred to exist from its activities, such negative concepts define it well. One would learn thereby that the soul is incomprehensible to the senses, without weight, size, dimension, location, or any of the qualities of matter.[19]

St. Gregory objects that such an analogy equates the soul with the divine essence. St. Macrina rejects the soul being *the same as* the divine essence as impious. The soul, however is *like* the divine essence since it is created in the image of the divine essence.[20] Since the soul is an image, it must be similar to its archetype in all things. The likeness of the intellectual is intellectual. The likeness of the bodiless is bodiless. Yet the soul differs from its archetype in the peculiar qualities of its own nature.[21] An image would be no image if it were the same as the original in all respects. But in the comparative smallness of its own nature, the soul reflects the properties of the divine nature much as a shard of glass reflects the globe of the sun, not according to the magnitude of the sun itself, but as the shard's limited size allows. Hence the analogy of the soul and the divine essence stands.[22]

What does one learn form this analogy? Due to the ineffable wisdom of God which is manifest in the universe, one can be confident that the divine nature and power is in everything that exists so that everything remains in existence. Yet the divine nature is totally different from the nature of any created thing. This dissimilarity in essence, however, does not prevent God from being in all things. Likewise, the utter dissimilarity between the soul's simple and invisible nature and the complex and solid nature of the body does not prevent the soul from dwelling in it. Although one does not understand *how* this is the case, it is hardly incredible *that* it is the case.[23]

The soul, although totally unlike the body in essence, still dwells in it and vivifies it while the body is alive. It coalesces with the union of the bodily elements. But when the body is dissolved in death and its elements return to their own, the soul does not perish with it. Due to its intellectual and dimensionless nature, the soul does not dissolve but survives and remains attached to all the elements which were once crafted into its body. Being dimensionless, the soul is neither contracted nor dispersed as are dimensional things. Hence nothing prevents the soul from remaining present with all of natural elements of its former body, regardless of how they are dispersed. So even in death the soul survives in union with the body's elements. What sadness is there in this? Why then should one fear death?[24]

If the soul is an intellectual and vivifying essence, how, St. Gregory wonders, does one account for such emotions as anger and desire in the human being? Both seem to be impulses of the soul. They do not arise from the body. So it must follow that they are intellectual. Since the soul has been defined as intellectual in essence, two absurdities arise: a) that each faculty, such as anger, desire, and so forth are each individual souls in us, or b) not even the faculty of thought in us may be considered a soul. He fears that the proposed definition of the soul either defeats itself and proves man to be soulless, or that it implies the ridiculous notion of multiple souls in man corresponding to each faculty.[25]

St. Macrina acknowledges that these faculties are generally recognized to appear in the soul. Reason alone, however, has not resolved their exact relationship to the soul, i.e., whether they are with the soul from the beginning or are added later. Hence most people remain in doubt about these issues and have formed no stable opinions about them. She foregoes free philosophical speculation concerning the soul and affirms Holy Writ as the canon and rule of all doctrine. With this she rejects Plato's analogy of the charioteer guiding two unequal steeds, Aristotle's assertion of the mortality of the soul, and the pre-Socratics, whom she notices occasionally expressed their views in verse (as did the Eleatic philosopher, Parmenides, born c. 510 BC).[26]

St. Macrina asserts that since the soul is an image of the divine essence, one should not attribute to the soul what is not also proper to the divine essence. Since desire and anger are alien to the divine nature, they must also be alien to the soul as well. She cites the example of Moses, a man supposedly free of anger and desire due to his meekness.[27] Since this example shows that a man may be separated from these things without harm, they must be not be essential to the soul but accidental to it.[28]

Furthermore, when distinguishing the essence of a thing one must focus on what is unique to it, not on characteristics shared with other natures. Anger and desire are common both to the rational nature of the soul and the irrational nature of the animals. These characteristics are thus inessential to the soul. The appearance of these things in the soul, therefore, do not upset the definition of the soul as intellectual and vivifying.[29]

Emotions are in the soul but are not of the soul. What then is their relationship to it? They are grafted onto the edges of the soul. How does this happen? St. Macrina proposes that Genesis 1 presents a certain ordered narration culminating in the creation of rational man. Of all creation, whatever exists is either wholly intellectual (i.e., the angels) or is corporeal. Of the corporeal creation some are inanimate, while the rest are animate or living, partaking in nourishment and growth. Of the animate creation, all of which shares in nourishment and growth, plants lack sense-perception whereas animals and man perceive. But of the creation which partakes in sense-perception, only man is rational. The life of sense-perception could not exist outside of matter, nor could intellect enter a body unadorned with sense-perception. So Holy Writ narrates the creation of man last. Man encompasses all forms of life. From the vegetative forms of life man receives appetite, nourishment and growth. From the animate but irrational creation man receives sense-perception and the ability to regulate himself accordingly. In corporeal creation, however, reason and thought are unique to man and thus distinguish his nature. But when the rational soul of man associates with the bodily faculties of sense-perception, it also associates with their traits, producing the emotions.[30]

These emotions on the boundaries of the soul are not maladies but indifferent morally. They can be directed by the will either for good or ill. If reason, which is characteristic of human nature and the soul, gains the upper hand and rules over the traits added from outside, none of these emotions would lead toward evil.[31] For example, fear would lead to obedience, anger to courage, and desire to divine and immortal pleasure. But should the soul lose its grip and fail to control these impulses, as a charioteer loses control of his horses,[32] they become passions. As the passions negate the strengths of animal creation, humanity dominated by them changes from intelligence and godliness to irrationality and mindlessness. By the force of these passions men become beasts. Thus the emotions grow on the surface of the soul. If used poorly they become destructive passions. If used well, as with Daniel's desires[33] and the anger of Phineas,[34] they are praiseworthy and can be useful in human salvation.[35]

The Soul after Death

Returning to the subject of the soul remaining with the bodily elements after death, St. Gregory asks how this notion fits together with the commonplace notion that Hades is a subterranean locale which serves as a receptacle for souls after death? If Hades is a location wherein souls dwell after death, how can they remain also with their bodily elements? St. Macrina asserts that Hades' essential meaning is that the soul after death is transferred to the realm of the invisible. But given the spherical shape of the earth, the air girding the earth about, and the sun's rotation around it so that wherever the sunlight shines the other side is dark, a geographical understanding of Hades seems implausible. But one need neither affirm nor deny such a view as long as he affirms the immortality of the soul.[36]

St. Gregory then cites Philippians 2:10, "that at the name of Jesus every knee should bow, of things in heaven, and things in earth, and things under the earth;" in support of the notion that Hades is a geographical location, namely that the "things under the earth" would be the beings in Hades. St. Macrina applies a more spiritual interpretation to this verse. The three places cited in the verse refer not to three locations, rather to the three states in which rational beings exist. Those in heaven correspond to the angels who have always enjoyed the bodiless life. Those on earth refer to embodied human souls while those under the earth are souls released from the body by death. As a result, this verse in no way compels one to adopt the notion that Hades is some subterranean location, especially when one takes into account the astronomical notions which St. Macrina previously discussed.[37]

If in life, St. Gregory wonders, the soul becomes accustomed to the bodily elements in the form of the body, what sign will remain after that body's dissolution in death so that the soul may continue to recognize these elements? The form being dissolved, what will distinguish the body's elements from like substances which were never associated with the body in question? St. Macrina presents two analogies: **a)** the mixing and unmixing of paints, and **b)** pottery sherds and clay. The artist knows the pigments from which certain colors are mixed. Were it possible for the original hues to be re-extracted from the mixed color and to return to their own hues, certainly the artist would remember the mixed color and would still know how to create it again out of the original hues. Likewise the soul would know through its cognitive power the elements of its former body and would adhere to them until the same body was drawn together again from the elements. Likewise, if a potter should make different types of earthen vessels, even for different owners, these owners could distinguish their own vessels while whole and even when broken. Should the pottery sherds be mixed in with unworked clay, the sherds would be easily distinguishable from the clay. Likewise the soul knows its own body when it coheres in its living form, but is not deceived as to which elements belongs to its body after death because of the signs and traces which persist in the remnants.[38]

This broaches the definition of the Resurrection. Should one object that it is impossible to re-create the same person in the Resurrection, the watchfulness of the soul over its bodily elements provides an answer. Should not the same but similar elements of the same substances be rewoven into the form of the original person, it would not be the same person resurrected, rather a new one created since the exact same elements were not used. But the soul's dimensionless nature allows it to adhere to its bodily elements regardless of their dispersal. Its intellectual power enables it to recognize its own. So when the power that rules the universe sends the signal to the elements to gather once again, then, by the one power of the soul, these elements will be drawn together once more. The reweaving of the same elements by God's command into the same living body through the power of the soul is the proposed definition of the Resurrection. St. Macrina uses an analogy of a rope and its fibres to illustrate this point.

> *In the concurrence of its own elements the rope of our body will be braided by the soul. Each element in order will be woven again to its former accustomed place and will wrap around that which is familiar to it.*[39]

St. Gregory accepts these proposals, but then questions how one would respond to the objection that the narrative of the Rich Man and Lazarus fails to agree with it due to its seeming attribution of location and physicality to Hades and Paradise?[40] St. Macrina replies that although the narrative does use corporeal terms, it still scatters many clues which suggest a subtler interpretation. If the eyes of the Rich Man remain in his tomb, which eyes does he lift up in Hades? How does his bodiless soul feel fire? What sort of tongue would be cooled by the water's drop and what sort of finger would administer it? What sort of chasm could separate the Rich Man from Lazarus since the intellectual nature of the mind goes instantaneously wherever it wishes? The barrier is not a physical gap but a barrier separating incompatible things.[41]

The key to unlocking the deeper mysteries of this narrative are seen when Abraham admonishes the Rich Man that he had already received the good things due him in his earthly life whereas Lazarus received his evils in his bodily life. Only at this point is the chasm mentioned. In this St. Macrina sees a great doctrine. Before the Fall, human life was uniform, partaking only in the good. Only that which contained opposites, the Tree of Knowledge of Good and Evil, was forbidden man and the penalty for eating it was death. But man in his free will chose to forsake the life unmixed with evil when he took to himself the life compounded of opposites. God, however, provided an opportunity for rectification.

Death would divide our lives in twain, into a brief bodily

period now and into an eternal period hereafter. God, in His love for man, granted man the choice where he would receive good or evil, either in the short temporal period or in the everlasting hereafter.[42]

Those who believe that whatever pleases sensation is good and whose reason does not recognize virtue, live their present lives gluttonously, leaving none of their good portion for eternity. Those who manage their lives with reason and self-control are distressed by misfortunes here, but save the better portion for eternity. So the gulf consists of the impassible logical necessity created by the choices made in this life. One who pursues pleasure in this life without repentance makes the land of good inaccessible to him throughout eternity. The bosom of Abraham becomes the calm harbor of refuge for those who sailed virtuously in this life.[43] The tormenting flame consists of the deprivation of the things which the worldly soul considers good. This worldly soul is needy but cannot partake of the good things swirling around the righteous. All these corporeal images therefore point to subtler spiritual truths. Hades therefore is not some geographical place, rather an invisible and incorporeal condition of life in which the soul lives.[44]

The narrative of the Rich Man and Lazarus reveals another doctrine, that of the soul's purification. This is seen in Lazarus being occupied with current circumstances while the Rich Man is preoccupied with his former life and family. The soul of the latter is still attached to flesh and blood. Hence the Lord teaches that while still living in this life one should free himself from the domination of the flesh as much as possible through the life of virtue. By doing so, the journey of the soul toward the good becomes light and easy, without the encumbrance of fleshly preoccupations hindering it.[45]

Should one, however, lead a very carnal life in the present, once dead and out of the flesh he will remain attached its experiences, much as a someone who works in foul-smelling places retains a stench even when venturing out into fresh air. His partially materialized soul would increase his torment in the after-life. St. Macrina cites Socrates' reference to ghosts in the *Phaedo* loitering about their graves in support of her notion of partially materialized souls. If this is indeed the case, it would indicate that these souls have become far too attached to the fleshly life and are unwilling to fly cleanly away, refusing even to shed the bodily shape and form after it has been dissolved.[46]

St. Gregory objects that if every irrational impulse is quenched after spiritual purification takes place, even the impulse of desire will be removed. Whence then comes any yearning for the better? Does this not go against the good consequences of using the emotions properly? St. Macrina replies that contemplation and discernment are proper to the godlike part of the soul since by them one contemplates the divine. So even after separation from the emotive faculties due to purification, the soul will not be hindered in its contemplation of the beautiful since in its own nature beauty has an attractiveness for its beholders. The divine is beautiful by its own nature and the soul, once cleansed of evil, will exist entirely in beauty. The soul will therefore be joined with the divine through its purity, adhering to what is proper to it. Once this occurs, there would be no more need to desire the beautiful since the beautiful would already be attained. Attainment therefore obviates desire. The soul in no way will be hindered from the good. Being an image of the divine, it will ponder its own beauty within and thereby behold its archetype as through an image.[47]

Since our nature is currently impoverished of the beautiful, it always reaches out for what it needs, using memory and shame to help it toward the good and away from evil. This yearning consists of the desiring faculty of our current nature, which either attains to the beautiful or is waylaid by some misconception of the good.[48] But the nature which exceeds every good conception and surpasses every power is itself the fullness of good things. It does not participate in the nature of beauty but is the nature of beauty and thus does not need such faculties. Since the divine nature surpasses every good and the good is dear to what is good, it desires what it has and has what it wants, needing and receiving nothing outside of itself.

But nothing is outside of it, except evil which is the

deprivation of the good.[49]

Since the soul becomes godlike once it has put off the impulses of its nature (or more precisely, the impulses grafted onto its nature) and enters into what it previously desired, they become superfluous. The soul even puts aside hope and memory since it is currently occupied with the enjoyment of the good things previously desired. The soul imitates the superior life, being conformed to the properties of the divine nature. Nothing is left to it but the disposition of love, which is the interior attachment to that which is good.

> *So when the soul which has become simple and uniform and an accurate image of God finds that truly simple and immaterial good, the one thing which is really lovable and desirable, it attaches itself to it and combines with it through the impulse and operation of love. It conforms itself to that which is always being grasped and found, and becomes through its likeness to the good that which the nature is in which it participates.*[50]

Since the soul will have attained what it had desired, it will no longer need the desiring faculty. St. Macrina cites the Apostle Paul in support of this notion when he states that love will survive such activities as prophecy and knowledge. Even when faith, hope and love are cited as abiding, the greatest of these is love since hope acts only as long as the thing desired is not present while faith provides support for such hope. For this reason love has the primacy among the virtues and among the commandments of the Law.[51] Should the soul reach its goal and embrace the fullness of existing things and preserve in itself solely the impression of divine blessedness, it will have no need of the emotive faculties. For the life of the divine nature is love, and the beautiful is lovable to those who know it and the divine nature knows itself and the soul communes with it. Satiety will not cut off the attachment of love so the divine life will always operate through love. There is no limit to the operation of love since the beautiful, which is truly lovable, is without limit.[52] The limitless operation of love which is due to the infinity of God reminds one of the limitless ascent to God asserted in *The Life of Moses.*

> *This truly is the vision of God: never to be satisfied in the desire to see him. But one must always, by looking at what he can see, rekindle his desire to see more. Thus, no limit would interrupt the growth in the ascent to God, since no limit to the Good can be found nor is the increasing of the desire for the Good brought to an end because it is satisfied.*[53]

Why then is purification painful? God draws to Himself that which is His own. So the image, which is soul, is drawn to its archetype. If the soul is light and simple, with no bodily weight holding it down, its progress toward the One Who attracts it is light and easy. But should the soul be attached to the bodily condition with nails of passionate attachment, it will probably experience what happens to bodies torn from wreckage. They will be torn and experience pain. Rope caked with mud proceeds through a narrow pipe only with forceful pulling. Likewise, goldsmiths purifying gold must melt the metal to rid it of impurities. Therefore the process of purification is painful. Punishment or vengeance, however, is not the purpose of this pain. Pain instead is incidental to the process of purification, the measure of pain being proportional to the quantity of evil in each person. Once all evil has been removed, and that which does not really exist actually ceases to exist, all choice will be in God. Evil will no longer exist since, with free will no longer choosing it, evil will have no receptacle.[54]

One must take care, therefore, to keep his soul entirely free from evil, or at least keep lapses to a minimum so that they may be easily cured. The Gospel narratives concerning debtors[55] indicate an exact reckoning according to the greatness of the debt and that restitution is not made by money but by torment. These reveal that by the pain involved in purification one pays the debt previously incurred by foolishly choosing unmixed pleasure in this life. Freedom comes, however, once the soul is cleansed from all that is alien. Those who are finally released from evil will be in the divine nature so that God may be all in all.[56] Humans will no longer need all the victuals, preparations and conditions which support life here since in eternity God will become everything necessary for us.[57]

But what should one say, St. Gregory asks, to those lacking the courage to bear their misfortunes? St. Macrina replies, essentially, that there is no use complaining about what is necessary, especially when one considers all the benefits which accrue as a result. God created man so that the divine goodness would not be idle. God thus created voluntary receptacles for souls which were created to receive the divine goodness. With the reception of the divine goodness, the receptacle becomes more receptive of the good since the good increases the power and magnitude of the recipient. Since the fountain of good things flows ceaselessly one grows endlessly in accordance. Therefore the person never stops growing in the enjoyment of eternal goodness. Ought one then grumble about the pain accompanying the path which leads to such bounties? Even if one is fond of the current body, it will be woven again from the same elements, but not with its current heavy and coarse texture. It will be respun into something subtler and lighter so that the beloved body will be restored in even greater and more lovable beauty.[58]

The Soul's Origin: The Soul's Destiny

In relation to the formation of the human body, when does the soul have its origin? Three options arise, namely a) after the formation of the body, *b)* before the formation of the body, and c) together with the formation of the body. Option A is dismissed immediately since soulless bodies neither move nor grow.

Option B is rejected due to the apparent absurdities and impieties which arise, namely those which arise from the concept of transmigration of souls. This leaves option C which is finally accepted.[59]

The transmigration of souls assumes that over many generations the same souls occupy different bodies, whether they be human, animal or plant. The Platonic, Neoplatonic and Origenistic traditions assume that souls are intellectual in nature and descended into physical bodies, a lesser order of existence, due to some sort of prehistoric fall.[60] St. Macrina categorically rejects any notion of transmigration of souls.

But, interestingly enough, she does not reject the use of philosophical literature entirely. The Christian accepts the teachings of the Church absolutely but may find philosophical literature useful insofar as it affirms the truth. The truth which the Neoplatonic philosophers assert along with the Church is that one day the soul will enter bodily life again. But where the Christian asserts this body to be the same body drawn from the same elements, the Neoplatonic tradition assumes the new body to be another one, be it human, animal or plant. The philosophers affirm at least, however, that the soul's reentry into the body is plausible.[61]

Option A above is dismissed summarily without further

discussion since St. Macrina thinks nobody is foolish enough to accept it. Rejected option B, which assumes the transmigration of souls, or in contemporary parlance, reincarnation, was accepted in Neoplatonic and Neopythagorean circles. So it is worth reviewing briefly why this is rejected. There are two possibilities here. The soul may migrate only between human bodies or between any kind of living body (human, animal, or plant). To avoid undue prolixity, some salient objections to transmigration between any type of body are listed below:

a) Each type of living being needs a soul of corresponding type. But transmigration confuses this by having one type of soul in many types of living beings.

b) Such views have obnoxious consequences, such as fear of consuming plants or animals lest they have human souls, or harshness toward humans due to the hardness engendered by consuming lower life forms possibly indwelt by human souls.

c) The inconsistent viewpoint that the evil descent begins in the heavenly realm whereas the soul's virtuous ascent begins in matter (assuming the spiritual to be good and matter evil).

d) The inconsistency of mixing the passionate with the passionless in that the descent to passion begins in the realm of passionlessness and the ascent to passionlessness begins in the realm of the passionate.

e) The impiety of assuming that all earthly life has its origin in evil, namely in an evil prehistoric fall, together with the idea's idiotic consequences. For example, since Spring brings much new life on earth does this season correspond to a special season of evil in heaven?[62]

The problem with transmigration between human bodies is threefold.

a) Human life is posited as having its origins in evil.

b) It too has idiotic consequences. For example, do souls hover over the marriage bed to snatch some newborn body? Does the wedding bed engender evil in heaven to facilitate a soul's descent into a body? What happens to souls which fail to snatch a body?

c) The transmigration of souls between human bodies undermines both the human potential for virtue and eliminates any meaningful providential oversight.[63]

This last point merits further discussion. If evil underlies human origins, how could man attain to virtue, or even desire it? A thing's end must maintain the character of its beginning, so an evil origin would preclude the possibility of human virtue. The fruit, after all, must spring from the nature of its seed. Even worse, such a posited origin of human life elevates chance and an automatic principle to the role of prime life-giver and ruler, displacing any meaningful notion of Divine Providence. If one's nature began in evil, how would developing virtue be of any benefit to it? Life would also be driven by mere chance, making virtue folly and eliminating divine oversight of human life. How could humans even begin to strive toward the good. Speech, for example, is not in irrational animal nature. So animals do not try to speak. If good is not in human nature, therefore, the ascent to good would be impossible since goodness would not be natural for man.[64]

But those who have purified their souls by reason desire the virtuous life. This common sense evidence clearly reveals that evil is neither older than life nor the first principle of human nature. Human life is directed by God as is the universe. God creates the human soul free from the necessity of evil, i.e., human nature is essentially good. Physical evil, namely the deprivation of some good physical quality, may come either by accident or by the exercise of human will. The constitution of the soul is from God, however, and thus is essentially free from the necessity of evil. Evil arises in the soul due to misinformed choice, whether by the darkness of deception or a plot of the enemy. But the soul may also look away from the darkness of deception toward the truth and away from the passions of darkness.[65]

So the notion that human souls existed before the body is rejected due to the issues described above. Since soulless bodies are lifeless bodies, nobody would assert that the soul is formed after the body. That leaves the third alternative, that the soul begins simultaneously with the coalescence of the body. Yet one may accept that the soul comes into being simultaneously with the body, but how this came to be is beyond the scope of reason. Citing Hebrews 11:3, St. Macrina asserts that even holy men found this question beyond their ken, and for good reason. Trying to explain the how leads to insoluble logical and theological problems, such as how moving natures arise from a stationary nature (the issue of the Prime Mover), and how composite natures rise from a simple nature. Such created natures cannot come directly from the divine nature due to the utter dissimilarity of their natures. But if not from the divine nature, whence do they rise since reason sees nothing outside the divine nature, i.e., before they were created. If something, such as matter, existed alongside God all along, this would imply multiple first principles. But all things have one cause, but are different in nature from the original creative nature. Hence two possible absurdities arise: a) assuming that creation is derived directly from the divine nature, one must attribute to the divine and uncreated nature attributes of created things, or b) positing some coexisting primordial matter alongside God, one must attribute equality in unbegottenness to matter since it too would be eternal. This clearly will not do.[66]

From this one can see why one should refrain from the troublesome question of how. But St. Macrina affirms the efficacy of the divine creative will, namely that

God can and did create all things. She asserts that the impulse of divine choice, when it wishes, immediately becomes a thing, its plan becoming a nature instantly. Nothing is very implausible concerning the creation of intellectual creatures since they are similar in nature to their creator. Corporeal creation, however, is apparently more problematic since the nature of corporeal things is very different from the divine nature. But concerning corporeal things, whatever appears in relation to a body, such as color, density, dimension, and so forth, is itself a principle, not a body. The concurrence and union of these principles create the body. Since these principles are perceived by the mind and not by sense-perception, and the divine is intellectual in essence, why could not the Intelligible One be able to create the intelligible principles by whose concurrence bodies arise? Therefore, how God created the soul and all things is beyond reason's ken, yet it is plausible that God created the soul and all things.[67]

Laying aside all questions of how the soul came into being, St. Macrina affirms third option that the soul came into being simultaneously with the human body, although one cannot behold all the faculties of the soul immediately. Using the analogy of the slip and the tree, St. Macrina discusses the maturation of the soul. As the tree growing from the slip is still a tree growing from a tree so, in the propagation of man, the soul-endowed human arises from a soul-endowed being, a growing being from a growing being. But as with nourishment a grain grows into an ear, so likewise as the human being is formed the power of the soul appears in accordance with its body's stature. In time, as a mature plant produces fruit, the human soul reveals the faculty of reason. Therefore both body and soul arise simultaneously and mature together.[68]

Logic, however, dictates that the number of souls will eventually cease to grow so that nature will not flow on forever and thus endlessly be in motion. St. Macrina proposes that eventually human nature will become stable and cease from generation when the proper fulfillment of intellectual creation arrives, since man is not dissimilar to the rest of intellectual creation. The need for generation assumes the lack of something. But when human numbers reach proper fulfillment, generation will cease. In the current condition, generation and corruption are inseparable. But with the end of generation a new condition will which will be without corruption. So it can be seen logically that the future life will be different from the current one, both being stable and indissoluble. When this fullness comes and generation ceases, the whole complement of souls will return once more from their invisible and scattered condition to visibility and unity. The same elements will assemble together again, returning to their previous order. Holy Writ calls this condition of life, "Resurrection," naming the whole elemental movement from their upward rising.[69]

St. Gregory affirms everything above but finds one thing

still lacking, i.e., a presentation of the doctrine of the Resurrection itself. St. Gregory then reminds St. Macrina of the many objections to this doctrine. She responds with an overview of scriptural texts which she finds germane to the subject.[70] But, St. Gregory objects, this was not the question asked since most of the hearers would agree on the basis of Holy Writ and the previous arguments that the Resurrection will take place at some time and that all will be submitted to the infallible judgment. He then cites further objections.[71]

St. Gregory sets forth four major objections concerning the doctrine of the Resurrection, all of which concern the nature of the resurrected body. Firstly, if the body raised will be the same in all respects, then given the travails to which the human body is subject, this would be a great misfortune. But if the body is not the same in all respects, the person is not resurrected, rather a new one is formed in his place. Secondly, given the fact that life is an ongoing process and hence is ever changing, what stage in one's life would be restored? For God to reconstitute all life stages, a person would have to become a whole people. Clearly this will not do. Thirdly, one's life often flows between self-control and intemperance, both of which operate through the flesh. Will the aged body be punished together with the lusty young body although the latter did not commit the sins in question? Finally, in our current life, nature supplies no superfluous bodily organs and parts. All provide functions needed for our survival in the present age. If all these functions are necessary in the hereafter, what good will have been the change? But if, for example, as Holy Writ says, one will neither give nor take in marriage, or need food or drink to sustain that future life, then the organs which facilitate these functions will be unnecessary.[72] Either they will not be present and our bodies will not be the same ones, or they will be present but superfluous. The first option is creation and not resurrection while the second is merely ridiculous. But Christians believe there will be a Resurrection and that such a notion is not absurd. *The point is how to make the doctrine of the Res-urrection plausible.*[73]

St. Macrina notes that St. Gregory presented several strong rhetorical objections against the doctrine of the Resurrection, none of which correspond to the truth. Indeed, those uneducated in the mystery of truth could be swept away by such forceful language into thinking that valid objections had been raised. Accordingly she refrains from answering in the same style.[74] The truth about the Resurrection is stored up in the hidden treasury of wisdom and will be disclosed only when the Resurrection taught by its actualization. Any speculation about the future condition of life now is as vain as midnight speculators pondering what sunrise will be like. The reality of sunshine will reveal clearly the vanity of these speculative discussions. But such objections ought not be left entirely unanswered, so she sets forth the aim of the doctrine of the Resurrection, its definition and its consequences.[75]

> *Therefore to describe this doctrine and limit it with a certain definition, we shall say this, that resurrection is the restoration of our nature to its original condition. In the first life, of which God Himself became the creator, there was presumably neither old age, not infancy, nor the suffering caused by the many kinds of diseases, nor any other type of bodily misery; for it is not likely that God created such things. Human nature was a divine sort of thing, before humanity started on the course of evil. All these things attacked us when evil entered our life. Therefore the life without evil will not need to be subject to the conditions which have happened because of evil.[76]*

Since the Resurrection is a return to man's original state, it sidesteps all St. Gregory's objections which assume a condition not to be restored. Resurrection life is to be the state God had intended, not what man made of it through choosing evil, with all its consequences. If a man should travel through frosts, his body becomes cold. If he travels through sunshine, he is tanned. But should one not travel through such conditions nobody would find it odd if he were untouched by the consequences of those states.

Likewise, when human nature became subject to the passions its life experienced the corresponding effects. But when human nature returns to passionless blessedness, it will no longer encounter the consequences of evil. When a man casts off a ragged tunic, he casts also from himself the ugliness that went with it. In like manner, when man casts off the dead and ugly garment made for us from irrational skins,[77] he throws off every part of his irrational skin along with the removal of the garment. All the things which come with the irrational skin, such as procreation, nourishment, growth, old age, disease and death, are removed together with the irrational skin. Hence all the conditions which underlie St. Gregory's objections do not apply to the resurrected life, avoiding all the absurdities involved.[78]

None of the conditions of the current life, including one's sins, will hinder God from achieving His goal, which is to set before everyone the participation of the good things in Him, of which St. Paul says the eye has not seen, nor ear heard, nor thought attained.[79] As. St. Gregory writes, *"this is nothing else, according to my judgment, but to be in God Himself; for the good which is beyond hearing, sight, and heart would be that very thing which surpasses everything."* Everyone will eventually participate in this. The difference in pursuing the life of virtue, or that of wickedness, would be in determining whether one would enjoy that blessed state sooner or later since the duration of the healing process corresponds directly with the amount of evil to be cleansed.[80]

St. Paul reveals the superfluity and ineptitude of the objections presented with his analogy of the ear and the grain in 1 Corinthians 15:35-49. Herein St. Macrina understands St. Paul to be rebuking those who limit

God's power by their own strength and understanding, imagining the future life in terms of the present. The kernel which falls into the earth and dies eventually rises and becomes an ear, which is neither totally unlike the kernel but is still not altogether like it. Between the two there is a definite continuity. The seed in the earth leaves aside its small size and particular shape but does not abandon itself altogether. While remaining itself, it becomes and ear which is different in size, shape, beauty and variety. Likewise, when human nature abandons in death all the properties acquired through subjection to passion, such as dishonor, corruption weakness, age differentiation, and so forth, it does not abandon itself either. Instead, it changes to incorruptibility, glory, honor, power, and every perfection. Its life is no longer ordered by its natural properties but passes over into a spiritual and immutable state. Of the excellent qualities shared by humans, animals and plants, none will remain in the life hereafter. Human nature lives on, but in a transformed and glorified state.[81]

Reason and Faith: St. Gregory's Theological Methods

As interesting as the content of *On the Soul and the Resurrection* is, the theological methods used by St. Gregory are equally noteworthy. The Cappadocian Fathers put a premium on a good secular education, but among them St. Gregory of Nyssa did so the most. His use of reason as a theological method is very pronounced in this treatise. His critical use of contemporary literature (mainly philosophical) in this work is much more apparent than is usual in Patristic literature elsewhere. In this treatise such literature is of *relative* value insofar as it is deemed true, truth being measured by the teachings of Holy Scriptures and the Church. As a result Holy Writ and teachings of the Church are *absolutely authoritative*. One must never forget that St. Gregory considered himself a theologian and not a philosopher. This section will therefore analyze how St. Gregory uses Holy Writ, the dogmas of the Church, secular literature, and reason in his construction of Christian theology.[82]

Holy Writ is an *absolutely authoritative* source for Christian theology. He proposes that *"the divine words are like commands, by which we are required to believe that the soul must remain forever."*[83] These words, *commands* and *required*, are very strong words, implying in an almost military level of acceptance. Orders are orders. Holy Writ is unconditionally true. Elsewhere St. Gregory sets forth authoritative scriptural revelation as a canon and rule of faith which is to be preferred over the ever inconclusive reasonings of the philosophers. Deductive reasoning is valuable, but Holy Writ is far more trustworthy.[84] What reason cannot determine on its own is made clear, when God reveals it in Holy Writ. Holy Scripture then is utterly authoritative for theology and immanently useful in that it cuts through the intellectual fog of rational uncertainty.

Being such an authoritative source Holy Scriptures are frequently cited, either as evidence for or as the source of St. Gregory's theological assertions. His assertion that the soul is similar in essence to the divine nature and thus is intellectual rests partially on his understanding of Genesis 1:26-27 wherein man is made in the image and likeness of God. Upon this assertion is based St. Gregory's proposal that the emotions are accidental to the soul, not proper to it.[85] St. Gregory cites Genesis 1 in support of his theological anthropology in that it supposedly narrates an orderly creative procession of life from plants (nourishment and growth), to animals (sense-perception), and to humans (reason and discernment). For him this illustrates the idea that the functions of lower life forms are prerequisites for the higher types of life. In this scheme man, as the highest form of corporeal life, encompasses all forms of corporeal life.[86] When St. Gregory rejects any conjecture concerning how the soul came to be as futile and beyond reason's ken, he cites Hebrews 11:3 in support of this, *"through faith we understand that the worlds were framed by the word of God, so that things which are seen were not made of things which do appear."*[87] Furthermore, his assertion of the perpetuity and superiority of the disposition of love rests on his interpretation of 1 Corinthians 13, Hebrews 11:1, and Matthew 22:37-40.[88] His doctrine of the purgation of souls finds support in his interpretation of Luke 16:19-31,[89] In short, St. Gregory enthusiastically acknowledges Holy Writ as fundamental to his theological propositions.

Not only does he cite Holy Scriptures as a source, but he must address them when they seem to contradict positions he would prefer, such as the notion that Hades is an invisible condition of life after death. Philippians 2:10 and the narration of the Rich Man and Lazarus in Luke 16:19-31 are proposed initially as evidence for the supposition that Hades is some subterranean locality. By reinterpreting Philippians 2:10, St. Gregory sets forth the "things in heaven" as representing angelic beings, the "things in earth" as embodied human souls, and the "things under the earth" as souls after death, in an attempt to show that this verse is hardly proof of Hades' physicality.[90] Elsewhere he points out that a literal interpretation of the corporeal imagery of the narration in Luke 16:19-31 quickly becomes nonsensical. But in these apparently nonsensical images he finds pointers to subtler intellectual interpretations, such as his teaching concerning where one may choose to experience one's good portion, and his concept of the purgation of souls.[91] Given Holy Writ's authority, any seemingly contradicting Biblical text must be addressed, in these instances by reinterpretation.

The teachings of the Church are also fundamental theological resources. In the context of the doctrine of the Resurrection St. Gregory asserts, *"but we say it is best to start from the teachings of the Church and to accept from those philosophers only enough to demonstrate that they are in partial agreement with the doctrine of the resurrection."*[92] The immediate controversy is the origin of the soul relative timewise to the coalescence of the body. Yet his method could not be clearer. When theologizing, one begins with the dogmas of the Church. Secular sources are useful, but only insofar as they are true. Their truthfulness should be *evaluated critically,* but the truthfulness of Church dogmas must be *accepted completely.*

If, however, secular sources are evaluated critically, they become valid theological resources, although of a secondary nature. They are valid to the degree that they are true, their truthfulness being measured by their concurrence with Holy Writ and the teachings of the Church. When they disagree with Christian revelation, they are not to be followed. St. Gregory, for example, rejects the materialist anthropologies of the Stoics and Epicureans since they are at odds with the Christian dogma of the immortality of the soul.[93] Concerning the nature of the soul and the emotions St. Gregory rejects the freewheeling speculation of the philosophers due to the contradictory and inconclusive nature of its results.[94] In proposing that the emotions are accidental to the soul, he rejects the Platonic concept of man's three souls, the appetitive, the spirited, and the rational, in favor of one soul which has the functions of Plato's rational soul.[95] He also rejects Platonic and Pythagorean concepts of the transmigration of souls in that they assume the soul to predate the body and, after death, to return to a body not its own.[96]

When the philosophers, however, agree with Holy Scriptures and the Church, they are accepted as useful allies. Although St. Gregory refutes the transmigration of souls, he accepts the Platonic and Pythagorean traditions partially in order to demonstrate the plausibility of the soul returning to an embodied state after death, a notion which he would strongly affirm.[97] When St. Gregory proposes that the soul of the Rich Man in Hades was overly attached to his previous life, indicating that the soul can become some-what materialized, he cites Socrates' discussion of ghosts in Plato's *Phaedo* to show the plausibility of his own interpretation of Luke 16:19-31.[98] In these instances, the role of philosophical literature is secondary since it is used in support of Christian dogma or of some argument St. Gregory would affirm. When used critically, secular resources are useful in Christian theology, although they are of secondary importance in comparison to divine revelation in the Holy Scriptures and the Church.

Philosophical literature is more influential in *On the Soul and the Resurrection* than merely making St. Gregory's propositions appear plausible. The literary format of this treatise is modeled on the deathbed discussion of Socrates in the *Phaedo*. He adopted much more than a literary genre from Plato. Platonic and Neoplatonic philosophical traditions informed his work greatly. St. Gregory's discussion of the soul, the body, the attachment of lost souls to their former lives and abodes are heavily indebted to these traditions.[99] St. Gregory's assertion of man as a microcosm of the universe was a commonplace notion amongst many Greek philosophers.[100] St. Gregory's emphasis on the mind as the instrument of knowledge, as opposed to unaided sense-perception, fits very well with the Platonic and Neoplatonic epistemological traditions.[101] St. Gregory's subjection of the appetitive and emotive faculties of man to the rational faculties of the soul are also very Platonic, although he does reject the Platonic notion of three souls.[102] When St. Gregory describes evil as a deprivation of good and posits evil acts and choices to be based upon misguided notions of the good, he stands clearly in the Neoplatonic and Platonic traditions.[103] His discussion of the nature of the beautiful is also much indebted to these same traditions.[104] St. Gregory's ideas concerning the natural attraction of the soul to the divine as the basis of the soul's purification and divinization is very Neoplatonic.[105] When St. Gregory criticizes the discipline of Hellenistic rhetoric as deriving its force from artful language rather than logic and truthfulness, he reflects the classical philosophical critique of rhetoric.[106] When St. Gregory found it amenable, he not only used classical philosophical literature to demonstrate the logical plausibility of his propositions, very often it influenced his theological ideas directly and powerfully.

The discussion above leads directly to another facet of St. Gregory's theological methodology, namely the role of reason in Christian theology. Like philosophical literature, reason's role is secondary to Holy Writ and the dogmas of the Church. Yet its role is considerable. The very purpose of this treatise was to reason out the doctrines of the immortality of the soul and of the Resurrection in order to demonstrate their logical plausibility. The purpose served by this demonstration of plausibility was to console the grieving. Since Holy Writ must be accepted unconditionally as a command, a certain support for the faith is lost since the mind does not voluntarily assent to the doctrines set forth in it. The reasoned presentation of the doctrines of the immortality of the soul and the Resurrection in this treatise is intended to compensate for that shortcoming.[107] Reason therefore strengthens the faith by demonstrating rationally the plausibility of its doctrines.

Reason can also clarify matters knowable to the mind, whether revealed in Holy Scriptures or discerned naturally. The clarification of Holy Writ is evident in St. Gregory's reinterpretation of Philippians 2:10 and Luke 16:19-31 in his discussions concerning the state of the soul after death. He also clarifies 1 Corinthian 13, Hebrews 11:1 and Matthew 22:37-40 in the context of discussing the enduring disposition of love and divinization.[108] His interpretation of Philippians 2:10 and 1 Corinthians 15:28 are foundational to his soteriological universalism.[109] Hidden things in the universe and in the human being, such as divine providence and the human soul, can be reasoned out and inferred, the first from the orderliness of the cosmos, and the second through the role of intellectual analysis in synthesizing knowledge from sensory data.[110]

Reason can also be used to demolish illogical and inconsistent notions as, for example, the transmigration of souls.[111] Whether revealed in Holy Writ or discerned naturally, anything knowable to the human mind is fair game for human reason.

Reason has its limits, however. If a subject is naturally inscrutable and is not revealed divinely, it lies outside the realm of reason. In Christian theology, such inscrutable issues are not to be addressed by reason since they are unknowable. One should accept, for example, that the soul came into being simultaneously with the body since the other options are inconsistent and often ridiculous. But how the soul came to be is inscrutable and not revealed by God.[112] These are realms into which reason transgresses at its own risk. At best such examinations are vain, such as any current speculation about the future condition of life called Resurrection.[113] At worst, endless logical and theological disasters await the mind overly bold in such matters. The mind must accept what is revealed and may analyze what is knowable to it.

Reason, however, must remain silent regarding what is hidden to it. Since St. Gregory is a Christian theologian rather than a secular philosopher, it is natural that he would set forth Holy Writ and Church dogmas as primary sources for his theological endeavors. In fact, St. Gregory is utterly unambiguous about their absolute authority in Christian doctrine. The prominent yet nsecondary roles of human reason and secular philosophical literature are reflective of the generally high estimation placed on secular learning by the Cappadocian Fathers, all of whom were Origenists. In this they reflect Origen's methods. Yet the degree to which St. Gregory esteems reason and secular learning exceeds the other Cappadocians and is one of the characteristic features of his thought. The literary modelling of this treatise on the *Phaedo*, although not unheard of in Patristic literature, is yet more evidence of St. Gregory's love of secular as well as sacred learning. Since *On the Soul and the Resurrection* was a treatise penned to make the doctrines of the soul's immortality and the Resurrection rationally plausible, reason and secular literature would play a greater role in it, the former being a method necessary to the genre and the latter providing much of the intellectual context. Yet St. Gregory need not have written a treatise about these doctrines in this format. The chosen genre and methods are in themselves revealing as to how greatly St. Gregory esteems reason and philosophical literature. The degree to which he does this distinguishes him among the Church Fathers.

St. Gregory's theological methodology has some very strong advantages. He has a clearly developed methodology. Holy Scriptures and the teachings of the Church are primary and authoritative sources of Christian theology. Secular literature, especially philosophical literature, is valuable as a secondary source if used discerningly, i.e., its truthfulness is measured against the absolute standards of Holy Writ and the Church's dogmas. Human reason is valuable in explicating matters within its grasp, either natural knowledge, or knowledge divinely revealed, as long as it remains silent about what it cannot know.

This combined use of Holy Writ, Church dogma, reason, and secular literature produces at times a very coherent and inspiring theological vision. Ones beholds this clearly in his soteriological teaching concerning the disposition of love and divinization. His sensible portrayal of Hades as an invisible condition of life after death is very agreeable to the modern mind. His ability to provide reasonable interpretations of Holy Writ, although often not modern, points the way to freer, although disciplined, means of analyzing Holy Scriptures without the intolerable intellectual bondage of literalism. Human reason is also given a very clear place in Christian theology, as long one limits its use to what God reveals and to what is otherwise naturally knowable. In St. Gregory's hand and mind, theology is frequently a more living, inspiring, free, and freeing undertaking than one often finds amongst the Church Fathers. Spiritually and intellectually, St. Gregory's theology is a waft of fresh air.

His methods are not without drawbacks, however. His argumentation can be dated as, for example, his insistence on the same bodily elements being rewoven to reconstitute the same person at the Resurrection. It can also be forced, as when St. Gregory proposes the plausibility of corporeal creation being created by an intellectual being since the former is derived from principles which by their nature are not corporeal but intellectual. His anthropology of soul and body are quite Platonic and thus not utterly modern, although such traditions still inform Western thought greatly. The coherency of his theological vision is sometimes overly strong, compelling him to overlook scriptural texts which do not fit, such as texts which reveal Moses' anger (Exodus 2:12, 32:19, and so forth) when he needed the meek Moses (Numbers 12:3) as evidence for the notion that the emotions are accidental to the soul. Even more serious, his strong Neoplatonic emphasis on the soul causes him to present the soul, not the whole human, as created in the image of God (Genesis 1:26-27). He also contradicts Genesis 1:28 when he views sexual reproduction as a result of the fall, although he is not alone among the Church Fathers in this assumption. Nonetheless this infringes upon the absolute authority of Holy Writ which he so strongly asserts.

His Neoplatonic intellectual leanings also constrict his theological vision somewhat. Although St. Gregory, for example, affirms the propriety of the resurrected body as well as some of the virtues of the current one, he fails to assign the body any soteriological significance. All such activities of any significance occur in the soul. In addition, St. Gregory's soteriological universalism is based as much on Platonic ontology as Philippians 2:10 and 1 Corinthians 15:28. When salvation is ontological to the degree St.

Gregory makes it, the notion of free will suffers since one cannot reject God finally. God will draw the soul to Himself regardless, eventually bending any recalcitrant will into compliance.

St. Gregory's theology, particularly his soteriology, has a certain unevenness unusual in Patristic literature. His soteriology often soars higher than the rest, but, perhaps like Icarus, a little too high for his own good. Nevertheless his work is a valuable theological treasure. One can derive much spiritual edification from his works, if read with discernment. But this is true of all the Church Fathers. No one of them is in himself an infallible guide to the faith, yet how impoverished we would be without them!

Endnotes

1. St. Gregory of Nazianzus never took possession of the see assigned to him by Basil, namely that of Sasima. He remained with his father in Nazianzus and, upon his father's death in 374, he took over administration of this diocese, but only for a short time.

2. The Arian emperor Valens died in the catastrophic battle of Adrianople (9 August 378) and was succeeded by the orthodox emperor, Theodosius I (ruled 379-395).

3. Johannes Quasten, *Patrology III* (Westminster, MD: Christian Classics, 1983) 254-255. See also *The Oxford Dictionary of the Christian Church* (ed. F. L. Cross and E. A. Livingston; Oxford University Press, 2nd ed. 1985) 599-600.

4. Johannes Quasten, *Patrology III* 255-56.

5. Gregory of Nyssa. *Gregory of Nyssa: Dogmatic Treatises, etc.* (ed. Philip Schaff and Henry Wace; trans. William Moore, M.A. and Henry Austin Wilson, M.A.; NPNF 5, Second Series; Grand Rapids, MI: Eerdmans, 1983) 430 (see note 1).

6. Johannes Quasten, *Patrology III* 261.

7. Gregory of Nyssa, *On the Soul and the Resurrection* (trans. Catharine P. Roth; Crestwood, NY: St. Vladimir's Seminary Press, 2002.

8. Gregory of Nyssa. *On the Soul and the Resurrection* 30-31.

9. Both the Epicureans and the Stoics had materialist anthropologies, Epicureans being atomists while the Stoics agreed with Heraclitus of Ephesus (late sixth century BC) that

fire was the primary substance.

10 Gregory of Nyssa. *On the Soul and the Resurrection* 31-32.

11 Or perhaps, "lifeless" since the Greek word for soul, *psyche* () also has the meaning "life" or "breath". This meaning would fit the immediate context well.

12 Gregory of Nyssa. *On the Soul and the Resurrection* 32. Christians and Stoics accepted the notion of divine providence in the universe. The Epicureans, on the other hand, accepted the existence of the gods but understood them to be too preoccupied with their own blessed state to attend to the universe.

13 Psalm 19:1-4.

14 A similar thought is expressed by Anaximander of Miletus (c. 610-546 BCE), see *Source Book in Ancient Philosophy* (ed. and trans. Charles M. Bakewell; New York: Charles Scribner's Sons, 1909) 7. See also C. Roth's note, Gregory of Nyssa. *On the Soul and the Resurrection* 34.

15 Gregory of Nyssa. *On the Soul and the Resurrection* 33-35.

16 Gregory of Nyssa. *On the Soul and the Resurrection* 37-38.

17 Gregory of Nyssa. *On the Soul and the Resurrection* 38-40. Concerning the citation of Epicharmus (Greek Comedian 540-450 BC), fragment 249, see C. Roth's note, Gregory of Nyssa. *On the Soul and the Resurrection* 38. [18]Gregory of Nyssa. *On the Soul and the Resurrection* 40-43.

19 Gregory of Nyssa. *On the Soul and the Resurrection* 43-44.

20 Genesis 1:26-27.

21 For example, the soul is originate while the divine essence is not.

The soul is finite but the divine essence is not, etc. [22]Gregory of Nyssa. *On the Soul and the Resurrection* 45.

[23] Gregory of Nyssa. *On the Soul and the Resurrection* 45-46.

[24] Gregory of Nyssa. *On the Soul and the Resurrection* 46-48. This perpetual union of the soul with the bodily elements after death is the intellectual foundation upon which St. Gregory will build his doctrine of the Resurrection. Interestingly enough, such sentiments seem reflected in the Orthodox Christian's strong aversion to cremation and desecration of the grave.

[25] Gregory of Nyssa. *On the Soul and the Resurrection* 49. St. Gregory seems to be raising and rejecting Plato's concept of three souls, the rational, the spirited and the appetitive. See Plato, *The Republic* (ed. Edith Hamilton and Huntington Cairnes; trans. Paul Shorey; *The Collected Dialogues of Plato*; Bollingen Series 71; Princeton, NJ: University Press, 1985) 676-685 (Book 4, 435-442).

[26] Gregory of Nyssa. *On the Soul and the Resurrection* 50. See also Plato, *Phaedrus* (ed. Edith Hamilton and Huntington Cairnes; trans. R. Hackford; *The Collected Dialogues of Plato*; Bollingen Series 71; Princeton, NJ: University Press, 1985) 493-502 (246-256.). Here she rejects the pre-existence of souls, their fall into bodies and much of the arising anthropology. She would reject any inference of the soul's mortality since she would prove the opposite, hence her disapproval of Aristotle. See Aristotle, *On the Soul* (ed. Richard McKeon; *The Basic Works of Aristotle;* New York: Random House, 1941) 556 (413A, 1-10). The pre-Socratic philosophers were usually materialist hence St. Macrina's dismissal of them. For an example of Parmenides' verse see Bakewell, ed. *Source Book* 11-20.

27   Numbers 12:3.

28   Gregory of Nyssa. *On the Soul and the Resurrection* 51-53.

29   Gregory of Nyssa. *On the Soul and the Resurrection* 52-53.

30   Gregory of Nyssa. *On the Soul and the Resurrection* 53-56.

31   St. Macrina sees this as implied in Adam naming the animal creation in Genesis 1:28.

32   St. Macrina alludes again to Plato's imagery of the charioteer and horses, but to illustrate her own psychology, which, in its emphasis on submitting the emotions to the faculty of reason is very Platonic, demonstrates that secular learning and literarature are not rejected but submitted to the discipline of Christian doctrine. See Plato, *The Republic* 4.435-442.

33   Daniel 9:23, 10:11, 19.

34   Numbers 25:6-15.

35   Gregory of Nyssa. *On the Soul and the Resurrection* 54-60. St. Macrina's understands the Parable of the Sower (Matthew 13:24-30) to contain useful doctrines concerning the proper ordering of the soul and the emotions. See Gregory of Nyssa. *On the Soul and the Resurrection* 58-60.

36   Gregory of Nyssa. *On the Soul and the Resurrection* 61-62.

37   Gregory of Nyssa. *On the Soul and the Resurrection* 63-64.

38   Gregory of Nyssa. *On the Soul and the Resurrection* 65-69.

39   Gregory of Nyssa. *On the Soul and the Resurrection* 68-69.

40   Luke 16:19-31.

41   Gregory of Nyssa. *On the Soul and the Resurrection* 69-70.

42   Gregory of Nyssa. *On the Soul and the Resurrection* 70-71.

43   The Greek for "bosom," can also mean harbor, hence the sailing and harbor imagery.

44   Gregory of Nyssa. *On the Soul and the Resurrection* 72-73.

45   Gregory of Nyssa. *On the Soul and the Resurrection* 75-76.

46   Gregory of Nyssa. *On the Soul and the Resurrection* 76. This whole discussion of the materialization of the soul shows very strongly the influence of Plato's *Phaedo.* St. Gregory's description of the natures of the soul and body seem heavily indebted to Plato. Furthermore, St. Gregory and Plato agree that souls attracted to the worldly life do not make a clean break with it and do not give up bodily qualities altogether. Concerning the outcome for these souls, however, Plato and St. Gregory disagree. Plato asserts that these ghosts, who would be the souls of the wicked, loiter around the grave and earthly places due to fear of Hades or of the invisible until their attraction to the flesh traps them once again in a lower life form. St. Gregory understands, in contrast to this, that such attractions impede the soul's progress toward the good and hence torment the soul in the afterlife. He does not really affirm the existence of ghosts and certainly rejects any notion of reincarnation. See Plato, *Phaedo* (ed. Edith Hamilton and Huntington Cairnes; trans. H. Tredennick; *The Collected Dialogues of Plato*; Bollingen Series 71; Princeton, NJ: University Press, 1985) 62-67 (79A-84B). See C. Roth's notes in Gregory of Nyssa. *On the Soul and the Resurrection* 75-76.

47   Gregory of Nyssa. *On the Soul and the Resurrection* 77-78. Again St. Gregory shows Plato's influence in associating the beautiful with the good and that one is beautiful through participation in

the form of the beautiful. See Plato, *Lysis* (ed. Edith Hamilton and Huntington Cairnes; trans. J. Wright; *The Collected Dialogues of Plato*; Bollingen Series 71; Princeton, NJ: University Press, 1985) 159-160 (216), also Plato, *Symposium* (ed. Edith Hamilton and Huntington Cairnes; trans. M. Joyce; *The Collected Dialogues of Plato*; Bollingen Series 71; Princeton, NJ: University Press, 1985) 553-554, 562-563 (201, 211). See C. Roth's notes in Gregory of Nyssa. *On the Soul and the Resurrection* 79.

48 Yet another Platonism, all men desire what they perceive as good and hence may miss the good due to misconceptions about it. Attainment of the good therefore requires knowledge of what is truly good. See Plato, *Meno* (ed. Edith Hamilton and Huntington Cairnes; trans. W. K. C. Guthrie; *The Collected Dialogues of Plato*; Bollingen Series 71; Princeton, NJ: University Press, 1985) 360-361, 373-374 (77, 88), also Plato, *Euthydemus* (ed. Edith Hamilton and Huntington Cairnes; trans. W. H. D. Rouse; *The Collected Dialogues of Plato;* Bollingen Series 71; Princeton, NJ: University Press, 1985) 394-395 (281).

49 Gregory of Nyssa. *On the Soul and the Resurrection* 78-79. Note the contemporary Neoplatonic notion of good as the deprivation of evil as, for example, in Plotinus *Enneads* 1.8.3, see Bakewell, ed. *Source Book* 375-377. See C. Roth's notes in Gregory of Nyssa. *On the Soul and the Resurrection* 79.

50 Gregory of Nyssa. *On the Soul and the Resurrection* 79-80.

51 1 Corinthians 13, Hebrews 11:1, and Matthew 22:37-40.

52 Gregory of Nyssa. *On the Soul and the Resurrection* 80-81. Here St. Gregory rejects Origen's notion that satiety with the divine goodness led to the prehistoric fall of souls into bodies. See Origen, *On First Principles* (trans. G. W. Butterworth; Gloucester,

MA: Peter Smith, 1973) 38-39, 66-68, 129-131 (1.3.8, 1.8.1, 2.9.1-2). See C. Roth's notes in Gregory of Nyssa. *On the Soul and the Resurrection* 81.

53 Gregory of Nyssa. *The Life of Moses* (trans. Abraham Malherbe and Everett Ferguson; New York: Paulist Press, 1978) 116 (239).

54 Gregory of Nyssa. *On the Soul and the Resurrection* 83-85.

55 Matthew 5:26, 18:24, 18:34; Luke 7:41.

56 1 Corinthians 15:28. This scripture passage and St. Gregory's ontological understanding of divinization, in which no soul is exempt from the divine attraction, form the basis of his universalism.

57 Gregory of Nyssa. *On the Soul and the Resurrection* 85-87.

58 Gregory of Nyssa. *On the Soul and the Resurrection* 87-88.

59 Gregory of Nyssa. *On the Soul and the Resurrection* 99-100.

60 Origen, *On First Principles* 1.3.8, 1.8.1, 2.9.1-2, also Plato, *The Republic* (ed. Edith Hamilton and Huntington Cairnes; trans. Paul Shorey; *The Collected Dialogues of Plato;* Bollingen Series 71; Princeton, NJ: University Press, 1985) 838-844 (Book 10, 614-621), and Plotinus *Enneads* 4.8.1-2, see Bakewell, ed. *Source Book* 384-389. See C. Roth's notes in Gregory of Nyssa. *On the Soul and the Resurrection* 89.

61 Gregory of Nyssa. *On the Soul and the Resurrection* 89-90.

62 Gregory of Nyssa. *On the Soul and the Resurrection* 90-94.

63 Gregory of Nyssa. *On the Soul and the Resurrection* 94-95.

64 Gregory of Nyssa. *On the Soul and the Resurrection* 95-96.

65 Gregory of Nyssa. *On the Soul and the Resurrection* 96.

66 Gregory of Nyssa. *On the Soul and the Resurrection* 97-98. The Greek philosophers, especially the Pre-Socratics, typically assumed the eternal pre-existence of matter.

67 Gregory of Nyssa. *On the Soul and the Resurrection* 98-99.

68 *Gregory of Nyssa. On the Soul and the Resurrection* 99-100.

69 Gregory of Nyssa. *On the Soul and the Resurrection* 100-103. meaning a "making to rise," a "rising or standing."

70 Psalm 103 (104 LXX): 29-30, 117 (118 LXX):27; Hebrews 8-10, Ezekiel 37:1-14; 1 Corinthians 15:51-53; John 4:46-53, and so forth. See Gregory of Nyssa. *On the Soul and the Resurrection* 104-108. For brevity's sake this section will not be discussed in detail.

71 Gregory of Nyssa. *On the Soul and the Resurrection* 108.

72 See Matthew 22:30; Romans 14:17.

73 Gregory of Nyssa. *On the Soul and the Resurrection* 108-112.

74 This was a standard philosophical objection to the discipline of Hellenistic rhetoric, that its force relied on persuasive and artful language rather than on logic, valid objections, and truthfulness. St. Macrina's refusal to use these methods would also be a standard response of a philosopher.

75 Gregory of Nyssa. *On the Soul and the Resurrection* 112 113

76 Gregory of Nyssa. *On the Soul and the Resurrection* 113.

77 Genesis 3:21.

78 Gregory of Nyssa. *On the Soul and the Resurrection* 113-115. These

irrational skins are defined as *the form of the irrational nature which we have put on from our association with passion.* See Gregory of Nyssa. *On the Soul and the Resurrection* 114. St. Gregory also understands the resurrected body to be rewoven into a finer subtler texture. See Gregory of Nyssa. *On the Soul and the Resurrection* 88. So the body is not discarded by the soul but changes its state in correspondence to the new condition of life. This seems very close to Origin's notion that the soul will always be associated with the body but that its characteristics are changeable, thus varying according to the condition of the beings whose bodies they are. See Origen, *On First Principles* 2.2.1-2, 4.4.8.

79   1 Corinthians 2:9.

80   Gregory of Nyssa. *On the Soul and the Resurrection* 116.

81   Gregory of Nyssa. *On the Soul and the Resurrection* 116-118.

82   ince the discussion now turns to St. Gregory's theological methods, and since St. Gregory used St. Macrina in this treatise as a vehicle to express his own theological propositions, all theological assertions in the treatise are attributed to him for the remainder of this study.

83   Gregory of Nyssa. *On the Soul and the Resurrection* 29.

84   This arises in the discussion of the relationship between the emotions and the nature of the soul, see Gregory of Nyssa. *On the Soul and the Resurrection* 50, 58.

85   Gregory of Nyssa. *On the Soul and the Resurrection* 45.

86   Gregory of Nyssa. *On the Soul and the Resurrection* 55-58.

87   Gregory of Nyssa. *On the Soul and the Resurrection* 97.

88 Gregory of Nyssa. *On the Soul and the Resurrection* 79-81.

89 Gregory of Nyssa. *On the Soul and the Resurrection* 75-76.

90 Gregory of Nyssa. *On the Soul and the Resurrection* 62-64.

91 Gregory of Nyssa. *On the Soul and the Resurrection* 69-76.

92 Gregory of Nyssa. *On the Soul and the Resurrection* 89.

93 Gregory of Nyssa. *On the Soul and the Resurrection* 31-32. See also above, p. 3, note 9.

94 Gregory of Nyssa. *On the Soul and the Resurrection* 50. Specifically, he rejects Plato, Aristotle and the pre-Socratics. See above, p. 6, note 26.

95 Gregory of Nyssa. *On the Soul and the Resurrection* 49-60. See above, p. 7, note 32.

96 Gregory of Nyssa. *On the Soul and the Resurrection* 89-96. See above, p. 12, note 60.

97 Gregory of Nyssa. *On the Soul and the Resurrection* 89-90.

98 Gregory of Nyssa. *On the Soul and the Resurrection* 76. See above, p. 9, note 46.

99 Gregory of Nyssa. *On the Soul and the Resurrection* 75-76. See above, p. 9, note 46.

100 Gregory of Nyssa. *On the Soul and the Resurrection* 34. See above, p. 3, note 14

101 Gregory of Nyssa. *On the Soul and the Resurrection* 31-32.

102 Gregory of Nyssa. *On the Soul and the Resurrection* 56-60, 70-73. See also Plato, *The Republic* 4.435-442, also above, p. 7, note 32.

103 Gregory of Nyssa. *On the Soul and the Resurrection* 78-79, 83-85, 96, 121. See above, p 10, notes 48 and 49.

104 Gregory of Nyssa. *On the Soul and the Resurrection* 77-81. See above, p. 10, note 47.

105 Gregory of Nyssa. *On the Soul and the Resurrection* 76, 83. See Plotinus *Enneads* 4.8.1-2, see Bakewell, ed. *Source Book* 386, 389-393.

106 Gregory of Nyssa. *On the Soul and the Resurrection* 112-113.

107 Gregory of Nyssa. *On the Soul and the Resurrection* 29, 112.

108 Gregory of Nyssa. *On the Soul and the Resurrection* 79-81.

109 Gregory of Nyssa. *On the Soul and the Resurrection* 85-87, 106-107. See above, p. 11, note 56.

110 Gregory of Nyssa. *On the Soul and the Resurrection* 31-35.

111 Gregory of Nyssa. *On the Soul and the Resurrection* 89-96.

112 Gregory of Nyssa. *On the Soul and the Resurrection* 97-101.

113 Gregory of Nyssa. *On the Soul and the Resurrection* 113.

About the Author

Brian Fitzgerald is an independent scholar, adjunct professor at Eastern University, and long-term Orthodox Christian with publications at Liverpool University Press, the Abdul Hameed Shoman Foundation, and the Annual of the Department of Antiquities of Jordan. He has special interests in Byzantine and Syriac Christian history and theology, as well as Roman, Late Antique, Byzantine, and Middle Eastern history in general.

Selected Bibliography

Source Book in Ancient Philosophy (ed. and trans. Charles M. Bakewell; New York: Charles Scribner's Sons, 1909).

The Basic Works of Aristotle (ed. Richard McKeon; New York: Random House, 1941).

The Collected Works of Plato (ed. Edith Hamilton and Huntington Cairnes; Bollingen Series 71; Princeton, NJ: University Press, 1985).

The Oxford Dictionary of the Christian Church (ed. F. L. Cross and E. A. Livingston; Oxford University Press, 2nd ed. 1985) 599-600.

Copleston, Frederick, S. J. *A History of Philosophy: Volume 1: Greece and Rome - From the Pre--Socratics to Plotinus* (New York: Bantam, 1993).

Cornford, F. M. *Before and After Socrates* (Cambridge: University Press, 1979).

Gregory of Nyssa. *Gregory of Nyssa: Dogmatic Treatises, etc.* (ed. Philip Schaff and Henry Wace; trans. William Moore, M.A. and Henry Austin Wilson, M.A.; NPNF 5, Second Series; Grand Rapids, MI: Eerdmans, 1983).

Gregory of Nyssa. *On the Soul and the Resurrection* (trans. Catharine P. Roth; Crestwood, NY: St. Vladimir's Seminary Press, 1993).

Lossky, Vladimir *The Mystical Theology of the Eastern Church* (Crestwood, NY: St. Vladimir' s Seminary Press, 1976).

Meyendorff, John. *Byzantine Theology: Historical Trends and Doctrinal Themes* (Crestwood, NY: St. Vladimir's Seminary Press, 1983).

Pelikan, Jaroslav. *The Christian Tradition: The Emergence of the Catholic Tradition (100-600)* (Chicago: University of Chicago, 1971).

Quasten, Johannes. *Patrology III* (Westminster, MD: Christian Classics, 1983) 254-296.

Staniloae, Dumitru. *Theology and the Church* (trans. Robert Barringer; Crestwood, NY: St. Vladimir's Seminary Press, 1980).

www.ingramcontent.com/pod-product-compliance
Lightning Source LLC
LaVergne TN
LVHW051709080426
835511LV00017B/2822